Le pı

MW01686838

Marie-Hélène Delval est née en 1944 près de Nantes. C'est l'habitude de lire des histoires à ses enfants qui l'a décidée à en écrire elle-même. Son imagination tournée vers la littérature fantastique l'a entraînée à peupler ses histoires d'ogres et de sorcières, mais aussi de petits enfants qui ressemblent à ceux d'aujourd'hui.

Du même auteur dans Bayard Poche :
Le pommier canoë - Rose cochon veut voir le monde -
La Moufette qui n'avait plus de maison - Les trois sorcières -
L'ogre qui avait peur des enfants - Un petit loup de plus -
Les deux maisons de Petit Blaireau - Éloïse et les loups -
Un petit frère pas comme les autres - L'école des géants -
Derrière la très haute montagne (Les belles histoires)
Les sept sorcières - Victor, l'enfant sauvage -
La nuit de l'ange et du diable (J'aime lire)

Serge Bloch est né en 1956 à Colmar. Il fait ses études à l'École des arts décoratifs de Strasbourg puis, après quelques années, il s'installe à Paris. Actuellement il travaille chez Bayard où il est rédacteur en chef de la revue *Astrapi*. Quand il lui reste du temps, il fait des illustrations pour les petits et les plus grands ; il adore aussi faire des dessins humoristiques. Ses ouvrages sont publiés chez Gallimard, Grasset, Casterman et Bayard Éditions.

Du même illustrateur dans Bayard Poche :
Guillaume le dernier - Rodogon le renard -
Surprise chez les Dupont (Les belles histoires)
L'atroce monsieur Terroce - Monsieur Boniface -
Mon copain bizarre - Monsieur Boniface rajeunit -
À nous deux, monsieur Boniface ! (J'aime lire)

Bayard Éditions est une marque
du département Livre de Bayard Presse

ISBN 2.227.72216.9

Le professeur Cerise

Une histoire écrite par Marie-Hélène Delval
illustrée par Serge Bloch

Cinquième édition

BAYARD POCHE

La ville du jeu

Le jour se lève à peine sur Loto-Ville. Le professeur Cerise est déjà debout. Il appuie sur un bouton blanc : clac ! le hublot de la cuisine soulève son volet. Il appuie sur un bouton rouge : clac ! le bras articulé de la théière-grilloir lui tend une tasse fumante et deux tartines dorées. Il appuie sur un bouton noir : clac ! l'audio-diffuseur s'allume et une voix enthousiaste retentit :

Chers auditeurs, bonjour !
Voici un nouveau jour pour jouer,
un nouveau jour pour gagner !
Vous avez perdu hier ?

Aujourd'hui, vous gagnerez !
Jouez, jouez, jouez !
Pour gagner, il faut jouer !

Clac ! Le professeur Cerise coupe le contact en rouspétant :
– Ah, crapette ! Encore ces bêtises !
Par le hublot de la cuisine, on aperçoit le dôme du Palais des Jeux qui miroite au soleil. Loto-Ville, c'est la ville du jeu ! Le Palais des Jeux est ouvert jour et nuit. On y trouve les machines les plus perfectionnées pour jouer sur les planètes, dans l'espace ou au cœur de la terre.

Tout le monde dit :

– Loto-Ville, c'est une ville fantastique !

Mais le professeur Cerise pense :

– C'est une ville de fous !

Le professeur Cerise est un vieux savant, spécialiste des cerveaux artificiels. C'est un original, il ne fait rien comme tout le monde !

A Loto-Ville, les gens ne travaillent pas, ce sont les robots qui font tout. Mais le professeur Cerise fait ses courses et son ménage lui-même ! Les habitants de Loto-Ville passent presque tout leur temps au Palais des Jeux. Le professeur Cerise, lui, n'y met jamais les pieds !

Pourtant, le professeur Cerise aime les jeux. Il a même chez lui des jeux très anciens. Ils sont en bois ou en carton, des matières qui n'existent plus depuis longtemps à Loto-Ville. Et le professeur Cerise rêve de jouer aux cartes, aux dames, aux échecs ! Seulement, il ne trouve personne pour jouer avec lui ! Evidemment, ces jeux-là, sans fusées ni missiles, ça n'intéresse personne à Loto-Ville !

Aussi, le professeur Cerise est-il décidé : il va se fabriquer un partenaire de jeu, un robot-joueur ! Et même, pour que ce soit plus amusant, un robot un peu tricheur ! Seulement, le professeur Cerise a un problème : « Fabriquer un cerveau de robot-joueur, c'est facile, mais je n'ai pas envie de jouer avec une machine », se dit-il. « Il faudrait que mon robot ait l'air un peu humain ! »

Tout en réfléchissant, le professeur Cerise sort de chez lui. Il monte dans son triporteur à propulsion et il s'en va faire la queue aux distributeurs automatiques d'alimentation. Devant lui, un robot-caddie qui attend son tour fait un bruit de casserole.

« Il n'en a plus pour longtemps, celui-là », pense Cerise. « Il est bon pour la casse ! Mais crapette ! Comment n'y ai-je pas pensé plus tôt ! »

Ça y est, le professeur Cerise a une idée !

SUPEP

Le cimetière des robots

Un nouveau jour se lève sur Loto-Ville. Bien sûr, le professeur Cerise est déjà debout. Clac ! le bouton blanc, clac ! le bouton rouge, clac ! le bouton noir. L'audiodiffuseur s'allume :

Chers auditeurs, bonjour !
Voici un nouveau jour pour jouer,
un nouveau jour pour gagner !
Aujourd'hui, au Palais des Jeux,
une nouvelle machine à jeux vous attend !
Aux commandes de votre astronef,*
affrontez une tempête magnétique !
Gagnez dix, vingt, trente millions !

*Un astronef, c'est un véhicule interplanétaire.

Jouez, jouez, jouez !
Pour gagner, il faut jouer !

Et clac ! Cerise éteint l'audio-diffuseur. Il bougonne :
– Des tempêtes magnétiques, maintenant ! Ils ne savent plus quoi inventer ! Deux ou trois imbéciles vont gagner quelques millions. Et demain, ils vont tout perdre ! Ah, crapette de crapette !

Le professeur Cerise pousse un soupir et monte sur sa terrasse. Il prend place dans son mobylo-planeur qui s'élève en ronronnant au-dessus de Loto-Ville.

Bientôt, le mobylo-planeur se pose devant un immense terrain vague. Le sol est entièrement recouvert de carcasses de métal tordu qui brillent au soleil : c'est le cimetière des robots !

Il enjambe les machines, il les examine une à une. Soudain, il trébuche : il s'est pris le pied dans une main de métal !

C'est une superbe main, avec cinq doigts, bien articulés, au bout d'un vrai bras avec un poignet et un coude !

– Crapette ! s'exclame Cerise. Un bras de robot-valet ! Exactement ce que je cherchais ! Pourvu que je trouve le reste du corps !

Des robots-valets, on n'en fabrique plus depuis longtemps à Loto-Ville. C'était un modèle de robot très délicat à entretenir, car les robots-valets avaient l'aspect d'un véritable être humain.

Le professeur se remet à fouiller avec ardeur. Soudain, il pousse un cri de joie : le robot est là ! Il a un vrai visage de métal. Des fils pendent à l'épaule, là où le bras est arraché.

– Ce ne sera rien à réparer, murmure Cerise.

Doucement, il prend le robot dans ses bras. Il l'installe dans le mobylo-planeur. Puis il s'assied à côté de lui et le regarde :
– Hello, camarade !

Le soleil se reflète sur le visage de métal. Et Cerise a l'impression que le robot sourit !

Il rentre chez lui très heureux sans se douter qu'à l'autre bout de la ville, un bien étrange personnage surveille tous ses gestes et écoute toutes ses paroles. C'est le terrible professeur Saturne, l'inventeur du télescope-microphone à écran.

Le professeur Saturne

Le professeur Saturne suit passionnément tous les gestes de Cerise sur son télescope-microphone à écran. Il le regarde installer le robot dans son atelier.
– Hé, hé, travaillez bien, professeur Cerise, ricane Saturne. Voilà un robot qui m'a l'air tout à fait intéressant !

Ça fait des mois que Saturne espionne Cerise. Comme Cerise, il était autrefois un savant très connu. Mais aujourd'hui, à Loto-Ville, on veut des jeunes, des spécialistes des machines à jeu ! Cerise, ça lui est bien égal. Mais Saturne est vexé et furieux. Pour prendre sa revanche, il rêve maintenant de gagner à tous les jeux et de devenir l'homme le plus riche et le plus célèbre de Loto-Ville.

Il se dit : « Un jour, j'entrerai au Palais des Jeux, et tout le monde s'écartera sur mon passage et m'acclamera, moi, le grand professeur Saturne, le meilleur joueur de Loto-Ville ! »

Mais jusqu'à présent, Saturne n'a jamais rien gagné. Et quand il entend l'audio-diffuseur répéter vingt fois par jour :

Pour gagner, il faut jouer !

il pense :
– Pour gagner, il faut TRICHER !

Aussi, depuis que Saturne a entendu le professeur Cerise parler d'un robot joueur et tricheur, il ne quitte plus son télescope-microphone à écran.

Cerise ne se doute de rien, bien sûr ! Il s'affaire dans son atelier. De temps en temps, il s'adresse au robot, immobile dans un coin :

– Tu verras, camarade ! Tu verras comme on s'amusera, tous les deux !

Et il rit tout seul.

Cerise travaille toute la journée et jusque tard dans la nuit. La lune éclaire doucement le visage du robot. Il a l'air d'attendre.

A minuit passé, le professeur Cerise achève la fabrication d'un appareil à peine plus gros qu'une orange. Il introduit l'appareil dans la tête du robot. Aussitôt, le robot se redresse.

Ses yeux luisent doucement. On dirait qu'il regarde le professeur Cerise avec amitié ! Il a l'air presque vivant !

Cerise est tout tremblant d'émotion. Il dit :
– Et maintenant, camarade, je te propose une petite partie de dames.

Il avance une table de jeu. Il pose sur la table une boîte plate en bois, avec des carrés noirs et des carrés blancs. Il donne au robot les noirs, il dispose devant lui les blancs. Et la partie commence.

Une heure après, le robot a gagné !
– Crapette ! Quel bon joueur ! s'exclame Cerise, ravi.

Il se met à bâiller.
– Bon, je vais faire un petit somme. A tout à l'heure, camarade !

Devant son écran, Saturne se frotte les mains :
– Merci, professeur Cerise ! Voilà exactement le robot qu'il me faut ! Il n'a pas arrêté de tricher et cet imbécile de Cerise ne s'est aperçu de rien !

Sur ces mots, Saturne éclate d'un rire diabolique !

L'enlèvement

Le professeur Cerise s'est endormi paisiblement. Soudain, il est tiré de son sommeil par un drôle de petit bruit :

– Bling ding badading cling.

Le professeur Cerise tend l'oreille. Le bruit recommence.

– Crapette ! Ça vient de l'atelier !

Il court jusqu'à son atelier, et ouvre doucement la porte. Il reste stupéfait.

Le robot a ouvert l'armoire. Et il avale une à une les boîtes d'écrous !

– Bling ding badading cling.

Alors le professeur Cerise se met à rire, mais à rire !

– Oooooooh ! J'aurais dû m'en douter ! Avec un robot comme toi, il faut s'attendre à tout ! Alors, tu es aussi voleur et gourmand ! Oooooh oh oh !

A propos de gourmandise, Cerise se souvient tout à coup qu'il n'a rien mangé depuis des heures, tellement il était occupé. Il ouvre un placard.

– Crapette ! Plus de saucisson ! Plus de cornichons ! Il faut aller aux provisions !

Le robot saisit un panier.

– Non, non ! s'écrie Cerise. Laisse, j'irai moi-même. Je ne lâcherai pas un farceur comme toi dehors ! Et puis, je ne tiens pas à ce que tu fasses des bêtises en mon absence. Alors, désolé, mon vieux, mais je vais te déconnecter jusqu'à mon retour. Voilà !

Sur le pas de sa porte, le professeur Cerise se retourne.

– A tout à l'heure, camarade !

Le robot est parfaitement immobile.

– Ma foi, reprend Cerise, si je ne savais pas que tu n'es qu'un robot, je penserais que tu as l'air triste.

Le professeur Cerise sort et il verrouille sa porte. Sur Loto-Ville il fait encore complètement nuit.

Cerise se dirige en chantonnant vers les distributeurs automatiques d'alimentation. Ce robot, quelle merveille ! Un sacré joueur ! Et, par-dessus le marché, tricheur, voleur et gourmand ! Il est vraiment sympathique, pense Cerise, tout attendri.

Il emplit son panier aux distributeurs d'alimentation. Puis il va jusqu'aux distributeurs d'outillage. Il ajoute à ses provisions quinze boîtes d'écrous.

– Pour ce fripon de robot, dit-il en riant.

Mais pendant ce temps-là, un mobyloplaneur silencieux a surgi et s'est arrêté devant la maison de Cerise. Un personnage enveloppé d'un large manteau noir en descend. Il projette sur la serrure un bref rayon vert, et la porte s'ouvre.

L'homme entre. Il ressort aussitôt, accompagné d'une autre silhouette, encapuchonnée de noir, elle aussi.

Tous deux prennent place dans le mobyloplaneur qui s'élève et disparaît à la vitesse d'un éclair.

Le plan de Saturne

Quand le professeur Cerise revient chez lui, il trouve sa porte entrouverte.

– Crapette, grogne-t-il. Il me semblait pourtant bien...

Il pousse la porte. La maison est silencieuse et vide. Le robot a disparu.

Le pauvre Cerise est désespéré. Il sanglote de tout son cœur !

– Un robot aussi merveilleux ! dit-il en reniflant. Jamais je n'en retrouverai un pareil ! C'est de ma faute, aussi. Mon pauvre vieux camarade ! Je n'aurais jamais dû te déconnecter ! Tu t'es vexé et tu es parti ! Mais que je suis bête ! Puisque tu étais déconnecté, tu n'as pas pu partir tout seul ! Quelqu'un t'a enlevé ! On m'a volé mon robot !

Le professeur Cerise ne pleure plus. Il est maintenant dans une colère épouvantable !

– Voler mon robot ! Si je tenais celui qui a fait ça ! Mais qui est-ce ? Qui peut avoir besoin d'un robot aussi spécial ?

Il fronce les sourcils et réfléchit profondément.

Pendant ce temps, le professeur Saturne est rentré chez lui avec le robot. Il le contemple avec un mauvais sourire, puis il ricane :

– Hé hé ! je vais te reconnecter, voleur d'écrous !

Le robot reprend son air presque vivant. Il y a même au fond de ses yeux une drôle de petite lueur, mais Saturne ne s'en aperçoit pas.

– Ha ha ha ! le merveilleux robot du professeur Cerise ! Nous allons faire des choses étonnantes, tous les deux ! Et l'homme le plus riche et le plus puissant de Loto-Ville, ce sera moi, le grand Saturne !

Le robot ne bouge pas, mais ses yeux luisent toujours.

– Tu veux savoir comment je vais m'y prendre, hein, robot ? Eh bien, vois-tu, nous allons désormais passer beaucoup de temps dans ce merveilleux Palais des Jeux. Ah ah ah !

Les yeux du robot brillent de plus en plus. Mais Saturne ne remarque rien.

– Écoute, écoute bien, robot tricheur ! A partir de maintenant, tu viendras tous les jours avec moi au Palais des Jeux. Au milieu de toutes ces machines de métal, personne ne fera attention à toi. Et tu joueras à ma place et tu tricheras, puisque tu triches si bien ! Et tu gagneras… ou plutôt je gagnerai !

Les yeux du robot brillent maintenant comme des lampes. Mais Saturne continue :

– Tous les jours, je jouerai et, grâce à toi, tous les jours je gagnerai ! Et bientôt, tout le monde connaîtra le nom du meilleur joueur de Loto-Ville, le riche, le puissant, l'incomparable professeur Saturne !

Il se passe alors quelque chose d'incroyable : le robot se met à rire !

Le robot joue et gagne

Le robot rit en cliquetant et en secouant ses épaules de métal.

– Et alors, hurle Saturne, j'ai dit quelque chose de drôle ?

Le robot cesse de rire. Et la lumière qui danse dans ses yeux se fait soudain menaçante. A pas lents, il s'approche et Saturne se sent brusquement inquiet.

– Bon, bon, robot ! Tu as raison de rire, après tout ! Entre tricheurs, on se comprend, hein ?

Mais le robot avance, les yeux luisants. Saturne recule en répétant :

– Allons, tiens-toi tranquille ! Sois sage !

Le robot avance encore. Maintenant, Saturne a peur. Le robot avance toujours. Il lève ses deux bras de métal. Alors, soudain,

Saturne panique : il saute par un hublot ouvert et se met à courir dans la rue comme un fou.

Il court, il court, bousculant les robots-caddies qui circulent sur le trottoir. Enfin, hors d'haleine, il s'arrête à un coin de rue. Il essuie son front trempé de sueur en balbutiant :

– Mais qu'est-ce qui m'a pris ? Ce n'est tout de même qu'un robot ! Il doit y avoir un mauvais contact dans son cerveau. Voilà, c'est tout bête ! Il faut que je vérifie ses connexions !

Mais quand Saturne se retourne, il voit le robot qui marche vers lui, en balançant ses bras articulés. Un instant, Saturne reste pétrifié. Puis il se remet à courir droit devant lui comme un fou, en criant :
– Déconnectez-le ! Déconnectez-le !

Le robot s'arrête et il regarde Saturne disparaître au bout de la rue. Puis il s'en va à grands pas.

Le soleil se lève, resplendissant, sur Loto-Ville, faisant briller la haute silhouette un peu raide du robot.

Quand le professeur Cerise voit revenir son camarade, il est si heureux qu'il lui saute au cou et fait sonner deux gros baisers sur ses joues de métal. Pour fêter ces retrou-

vailles, il décide de faire aussitôt une partie de bataille.

Là-bas, au Palais des Jeux, la foule des joueurs commence à arriver. Sur les machines, des lampes clignotent, des sirènes hurlent, des écrans s'allument. Cerise et son robot s'en moquent bien. Ils sont assis à leur petite table de jeu. Cerise distribue les cartes, la partie commence. Le robot remporte quatre fois de suite les cartes de Cerise avec un as.

– Crapette ! tu avais les quatre as ! s'exclame Cerise. Quelle chance tu as, camarade !

Il pose une nouvelle carte.

– Roi ! Cette fois-ci, c'est moi qui remporte, dit Cerise, tout joyeux.

Mais le robot pose un cinquième as !

– Ça, c'est trop fort ! D'où le sors-tu, celui-là ?

Le robot penche la tête. Vraiment, on dirait qu'il rit ! Il prend sous la table un paquet de cartes et le tend à Cerise. Il n'y a que des as ! Le professeur Cerise éclate de rire :

– Ah ah ah ! Crapette ! Le tricheur ! Le sacré tricheur !

Et il pose devant le robot une grosse boîte d'écrous.

Le robot hoche la tête. Il attrape la boîte et l'avale d'un coup :

– Bling ding badading cling !

Dans la série J'aime lire de Bayard Poche il y a plein de livres que tu vas adorer !

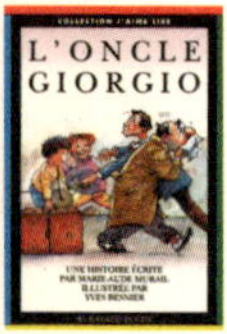

Des livres d'humour

***L'oncle Giorgio* (JL 10)**

L'oncle Giorgio est allergique aux enfants. Catastrophe, il est obligé de recevoir son neveu et sa nièce !

Écrit par Marie-Aude Murail et illustré par Yves Besnier.

Des livres fantastiques

***La bibliothèque ensorcelée* (JL 35)**

Ce vendredi 13, Aurore Coquille, la bibliothécaire, ne se doute pas que le livre qu'on lui demande va l'entraîner dans une véritable chasse aux sorcières.

Écrit par Évelyne Reberg et illustré par Maurice Rosy.

Des livres frissonnants

***Le mot interdit* (JL 6)**

Pas de mot se terminant en « eur ». C'est la règle du jeu. Un jeu qui peut devenir dangereux pour Thierry.

Écrit par Nicolas de Hirsching et illustré par Jean Claverie.

Des livres d'aventure

***C'est la vie, Julie* (JL 1)**

Ce matin, tout va mal, et Julie est loin de se douter qu'elle sera ce jour-là l'héroïne de folles aventures !

Écrit par Évelyne Reberg et illustré par Boiry.

Et n'oublie pas, dès 9/10 ans, les séries Je bouquine et Chair de poule !

Achevé d'imprimer en Juillet 1999 par OBERTHUR Graphique
35000 RENNES - N° 2348
Dépôt légal : Mai 1990 - N° Editeur : 4676
Imprimé en France

ABOUT THE DEVOTIONAL

It's the best time of the year! Christmas is almost here, and over the next 25 days, we get to spend time learning more about Jesus, why His birth is so wonderful, and what we should be thinking about as Christmas Day gets closer and closer!

You know that feeling of excitement and anticipation you have when you think about all the awesome things that Christmas might have in store? That's a feeling that many people in the Christmas story know very well! Isaiah. Mary. Joseph. John. The shepherds. The wise men. In fact, if you think about it, the whole earth was waiting for the moment that Jesus would come onto the scene!

In the same way, the days leading up to Christmas are a time when we get our hearts and minds ready to celebrate the moment that Jesus was born. And that's just what this book is for! Every day, you'll have a Bible verse(s) that focuses on a specific part of the Christmas story. Once you've read the verse(s), you get to read a message written just for you! There are questions after each message and an activity you can do with your family. How fun is that!?

You might notice a certain word come up a lot in the Bible verses you'll be reading over the next 25 days. That word is "behold," and when you behold something, you're paying special attention to a very important person or thing. That's what these days leading up to Christmas are all about – learning how we can focus all our attention on the most important Person ever, Jesus.

Christmas is a time for celebrating Jesus' birth because of how truly wonderful it is. That's where this book comes in. As you and your family go through *Behold the Savior*, you will learn how you can spend the whole month of December preparing to celebrate God's gift of His Son. If you have any questions about Jesus or how you can know Him better, make sure you talk to an adult who already knows Him. They'll be excited to help you!

MERRY CHRISTMAS!

DAY 1

BEHOLD!

Your eyes see things wherever you go. Sometimes, you look at things you've seen many times before and don't even think much about them. But then you see something amazing and gaze at it in awe because it's so fantastically wonderful. Not only do your eyes see it, but your brain also stops to wonder, and your heart feels astonished. You give that thing or person your full attention. There is a word that names this experience – behold. Behold means to be sure to see a remarkable thing or person. In other words, "Don't miss this!"

The next day he saw Jesus coming toward him, and said, "Behold, the Lamb of God, who takes away the sin of the world!"
- John 1:29

In John 1:29, John the Baptist sees Jesus and tells the people to behold Him. John didn't want others to just see Jesus with their eyes and miss out on beholding Him. Jesus was no ordinary person; He was God come to live on the earth as a man. John desired to make sure people understood just how glorious Jesus was. Through His life, death, and resurrection, Jesus provided forgiveness for sin and a way for people to become part of God's forever family. This is the most marvelous reason to **BEHOLD** Jesus, not only at Christmas time but every single day.

REFLECTION QUESTIONS

1. Why is Jesus worthy of your full attention?

2. What are some ways you can make sure you behold Jesus every day?

ACTIVITY

During these days leading up to Christmas, we will be focusing on the word "behold." To keep this idea in the front of your mind, as a family, create a sign with "behold" on it to hang somewhere in your house where everyone can see it. Make it bright and fancy to remind you that it means something extra special!

DAY 2
WHAT'S IN A NAME?

Did you know that names have meanings? Going back thousands of years, names were given based on things like events that happened close to a child's birth, special characteristics of the child, an important meaning to the family, or a purpose for the child. Most of the names that are used today have come from words in other languages. Some are very old names, going all the way back to Old Testament times. Your parents might have chosen your name because they liked how it sounded or what it meant.

For to us a child is born, to us a son is given; and the government shall be upon His shoulder, and His name shall be called Wonderful Counselor, Mighty God, Everlasting Father, Prince of Peace.
- Isaiah 9:6

Unlike most of us who have three names – first, middle, and last – Jesus was given many more! God was the one who was Jesus' name giver. Hundreds of years before Jesus was born, God told the prophet Isaiah things about Jesus. God shared some names that tell us a lot about what Jesus is like. A few of these names are listed in today's Bible verse. They are glorious names because they're all about the wonderful ways Jesus acts toward people. The best part is we can count on Jesus to always live up to the meanings of His names!

REFLECTION QUESTIONS

1. Why do you think Jesus has so many names?

2. What special names would you give Jesus?

ACTIVITY

Using your Bibles and computer, search for more of Jesus' names. (Make sure an adult supervises internet searches.) Look up the verses where these names are written in the Bible. Start with the 4 in today's verse, and then see if you can find 20 more and write each one on a small piece of paper. Put the papers in a jar. Starting today, choose one name each day to read and think about. Then, thank God for that wonderful name and what it tells you about Jesus.

DAY 3
A SPECIAL GREETING

Think about one of your best friends. Did you become friends because someone else told you to? Of course not! You became friends because you liked the other person, and they liked you. You shared some of the same interests. Once you make a friend, how do you treat them? You're kind to them, you show them special attention, and you give them your stamp of approval. In other words, you favor them because they're important in your life. You give it to them as a gift because of who they are.

In the sixth month the angel Gabriel was sent from God to a city of Galilee named Nazareth, to a virgin betrothed to a man whose name was Joseph, of the house of David. And the virgin's name was Mary. And he came to her and said, "Greetings, O favored one, the Lord is with you!"
- Luke 1:26-28

God sent the angel Gabriel to a young woman named Mary to deliver some astounding news. When Gabriel came, he didn't simply say, "Hi, Mary. How're you doing?" Gabriel greeted her in an extra special way by telling Mary that she was favored and God was with her. What a wonderful hello! God didn't send Gabriel to share His favor with Mary because He picked her randomly; He chose her for a reason. Just like you choose your friends based on who they are, there was something about Mary that God approved of – she followed Him and obeyed His laws. Because God saw Mary's faithfulness to Him, He chose to show her favor and bless her with an amazing purpose for her life.

REFLECTION QUESTIONS

1. What does favor mean?

2. What does it look like to show favor to someone?

ACTIVITY

To favor someone is to show gracious kindness to them. Talk as a family about ways you can show kindness to others — siblings, parents, neighbors, and even people you don't know. Maybe you could bake a treat and deliver it to a neighbor or pay for someone else's meal at a restaurant. Perhaps you could bless parents or grandparents by helping around the house without being asked. Maybe it's simply deciding to share smiles and greetings with people you see throughout your day. Choose one or two things your family can do for others this Christmas season to show gracious kindness.

DAY 4

NO NEED TO FEAR

Everyone knows what it's like to be afraid. Fear is that strong, very uncomfortable feeling we get when we think something could be dangerous or painful. There are many things that can make us feel afraid. Maybe for you it's spiders, big dogs, or the dark. No matter what the cause is, fear is a feeling everyone experiences. When you're afraid, you want someone to tell you everything is going to be okay, don't you?

> But she was greatly troubled at the saying, and tried to discern what sort of greeting this might be. And the angel said to her, "Do not be afraid, Mary, for you have found favor with God."
> - Luke 1:29-30

Whenever an angel appeared in the Bible, one of the first things he says is "Fear not." Having an angel visit you sounds amazing, but a big, strong angel suddenly appearing in front of you out of nowhere would be scary. When Gabriel came to Mary, she was troubled. She didn't understand his unusual greeting. God sent the angel to give Mary the most wonderful news, and He didn't want her to have any fear about it. So, Gabriel responded to Mary's deep concern and told her not to be afraid. Just like He used Mary as part of His plan to send Jesus, He wants to use us to share the good news of Jesus with others. And when He speaks, there's no reason to be afraid.

REFLECTION QUESTIONS

1. What are some things you think Mary was feeling when Gabriel came to her?

2. What would you want to hear if an angel came to bring a message from God to you?

ACTIVITY

As a family, find pictures from magazines or online of things that people might fear. (Come up with ideas that aren't terrifying to your kids to keep this project general.) Glue or tape the pictures in the center of a piece of paper. Draw a big circle around the pictures with a big line through it. Write on the top of the paper "Do not be afraid!" Use this as a reinforcement that we don't have to be afraid because God is with us.

DAY 5
A FOREVER KING

Some countries, like England, are called monarchies. A monarchy is a form of government led by a single ruler often called a king or queen. This ruler receives the position by being born into it and keeps it until the end of his or her life. If you were the oldest in your family and your father was king, you would become the next king or queen after he dies. Your child would be the next ruler after you. The kingdom, which is also referred to as the throne, is passed down from one generation to the next.

And behold, you will conceive in your womb and bear a son, and you shall call His name Jesus. He will be great and will be called the Son of the Most High. And the Lord God will give to Him the throne of His father David, and He will reign over the house of Jacob forever, and of His kingdom there will be no end.
- Luke 1:31-33

As Gabriel gives God's "don't miss this" message to Mary, she learns that she is going to have a son. He tells her that He would be an extraordinary baby. God was going to make Him King. Years and years before Jesus was born, God chose David to be king of Israel. David was an important king because he loved and followed God. From David's family line, generations later, Jesus would be born to rule just like God said. Where earthly kingdoms can be ruled by good or bad leaders, Jesus would be the very best kind of King—a forever king who is loving and just.

REFLECTION QUESTIONS

1. What character traits would make a person a good king or queen?

2. What makes Jesus the best King ever?

ACTIVITY

Using construction paper along with sequins, glitter, markers, or stickers, create crowns to wear. Take turns sharing things that a bad ruler might do. You could even pretend to be a king or queen and act it out. Repeat with things a good ruler would do. After that, talk about what makes Jesus the best King ever.

DAY 6

UNBELIEVABLE!

What would you think if someone told you that by the age of 10 you would win an Olympic gold medal for diving, be named the best race car driver in the world, and elected president? It might sound fun, but it's not possible. You wouldn't be old enough to participate in any of them because there are age limits. Also, don't forget all the money you would need to make just one of these things possible. And for one person, an adult or a 10-year-old, to win all three titles at once? For so many reasons, it just could not happen.

> And Mary said to the angel, "How will this be, since I am a virgin?"
> - Luke 1:34

After Gabriel told her she was going to have an extraordinary son, even more extraordinary than she could ever imagine, Mary asked one big question, "How can this be?" Mary wasn't married, and she'd never had a baby before. It wasn't even time for her to marry Joseph yet. It makes sense that Mary questioned the angel because she couldn't understand how something so unbelievable would happen. What she would find out next from Gabriel would explain how God would make it happen. Humans are unable to achieve the impossible, but God in His miraculous power can!

REFLECTION QUESTIONS

1. What are some other miracles God performed in the Bible?

2. What do you think would be impossible to do without God's help?

ACTIVITY

Try some of these impossible or nearly impossible things:

- Lick your elbow.
- Wiggle your ears.
- Move your nose without moving the rest of your face.
- Touch your nose or chin with your tongue.
- Tickle yourself.

These are silly things to demonstrate that humans can't do unbelievable things. Remember that only God can do the impossible!

DAY 7
MORE THAN POSSIBLE

And the angel answered her, "The Holy Spirit will come upon you, and the power of the Most High will overshadow you; therefore the child to be born will be called holy—the Son of God. And behold, your relative Elizabeth in her old age has also conceived a son, and this is the sixth month with her who was called barren. For nothing will be impossible with God."
- Luke 1:35-37

How cool would it be to build your own treehouse? Think of all the adventures and fun you'd enjoy! What if one day your parents said you could build one as big as you wanted? The only catch is you must make it without any supplies or tools. That would be impossible!

In the beginning of the world, God created all the plants, animals, lakes, mountains, the sun, the moon, and zillions of stars out of nothing! He just spoke, and everything came into being. When God created Adam, He used only dirt from the ground and His own breath. What's impossible for us to do is more than possible for God. Gabriel's answer to Mary's question, "How can this be?" was amazing. The Holy Spirit was going to create the baby she would give birth to. Yet again, God would do the impossible because nothing is impossible with Him.

REFLECTION QUESTIONS

1. What is a miracle?

2. Can you think of a time when God did something impossible for you?

ACTIVITY

You'll need an empty plastic water bottle and a balloon that's not blown up for this activity. Tuck the larger part of the balloon into the top of the bottle and stretch the edge of the balloon (where you blow into it) around the neck of the bottle. Try to blow the balloon up inside the bottle. What happens?

DAY 8
PUT GOD FIRST

Imagine a huge castle with dozens of rooms, lots of land around it, and kings, queens, princes, and princesses living inside. Because it's a lot of work to take care of a castle, the royal family who owned it would need servants. So, they would hire people like maids to clean and do laundry, cooks to shop for and prepare meals, gardeners to take care of the land, and guards to keep the castle safe. Having servants made sure that life in the castle ran smoothly.

> And Mary said, "Behold, I am the servant of the Lord; let it be to me according to your word." And the angel departed from her.
> - Luke 1:38

After Gabriel gave God's message to Mary, she responded with an important "behold" statement, saying she was the Lord's servant, willing to be used in His plan. Serving God is different from being hired to work in a castle. It means a person is humble, selfless, and wants to please God. Mary desired to set aside any importance she had. She wanted to focus on doing what the Lord wanted her to do more than doing anything else. Mary chose to love, serve, and obey Him without expecting anything in return. Being God's servant is the most important thing anyone can do. When we serve Him, it shows others how great and wonderful and glorious He is.

REFLECTION QUESTIONS

1. Do you think doing what God told her to do would be easy or hard for Mary? Why?

2. How can you show God you want to be His servant?

ACTIVITY

Fold pieces of paper in half. On one side, draw a picture of yourself. On the other side, write down (or have a parent write for you) some ways you can show God you want to be His servant. When you're finished, pray together, and ask God to help you hear His voice and bring glory to Him by doing what He says.

DAY 9

CELEBRATE WHAT GOD HAS DONE

> And Mary said, "My soul magnifies the Lord, and my spirit rejoices in God my Savior, for He has looked on the humble estate of His servant. For behold, from now on all generations will call me blessed."
> - Luke 1:46-48

When you hear the word magnify, a magnifying glass probably comes to mind. Using a magnifying glass gives you a close-up view of an object. It makes things look bigger. A microscope offers a similar view. It magnifies the smallest things you can't see with just your eyes and makes them appear large enough to get a closer look. Scientists use these tools in their work, and you use them in school. However, there's another meaning for magnify that appears in the Bible.

After the angel left Mary, she went to stay with her relatives Zechariah and Elizabeth who were also expecting a baby. When Mary greeted Elizabeth, something wonderful happened. The baby inside Elizabeth jumped for joy, and she knew that Mary's baby would be the Lord! Mary's heart was full of wonder, and she burst into song to magnify God. Magnify here does mean to make something bigger, but it's not talking about an object. It's about celebrating in praise and recognizing His greatness. When we think about who God is and what He's done, our response should be just like Mary's – magnifying Him and sharing with others that God is worthy of praise and is greater than anyone or anything in the world.

REFLECTION QUESTIONS

1. What are some words you can think of that would magnify the Lord?

2. When you magnify God, what does it tell others?

ACTIVITY

God is worthy to be worshiped for His character, promises, and the things He's done for us. Create a song as a family to give Him praise. Take turns reading (or singing) the song in the days leading up to Christmas.

DAY 10
A DECISION IS MADE

When a man and a woman get engaged, it means they've decided to marry one another. An engagement says they plan to marry each other. Before the wedding takes place, the woman or the man can freely decide not to get married. There are no laws that affect this decision. Today, the couple isn't officially married until the wedding takes place. At that time, legal papers are signed to make it official.

And her husband Joseph, being a just man and unwilling to put her to shame, resolved to divorce her quietly.
- Matthew 1:9

In Bible times, an engagement was called a betrothal, and it was very different from engagements today. When a couple was betrothed, it meant marriage was a promise. Before the wedding even took place, they were called husband and wife, but they didn't move into their home together until after the wedding. Joseph and Mary were betrothed when Mary found out she was going to miraculously have a baby. When Joseph found out Mary was pregnant, he decided to break their betrothal by divorcing Mary since the law allowed him to do that. There were also laws that would bring shame on Mary for having a baby before the wedding took place. Instead of reporting her for punishment, out of kindness, Joseph planned to keep the news of the divorce quiet.

REFLECTION QUESTIONS

1. Why do you think Joseph didn't want Mary to be punished?

2. Do you believe there are some decisions God doesn't want you to make because they're not His best for you?

ACTIVITY

Using popsicle sticks, colored paper, fabric, yarn, etc. make stick puppets of Mary, Gabriel, and Joseph. Put on a puppet show to tell the Christmas story so far. Each time a new character is introduced, continue creating the additional characters so you can have more shows as you learn more of the story.

DAY 11

GOD'S BETTER PLAN

At night, your brain creates stories you see in your mind called dreams. But did you know God can communicate through dreams? The Bible talks about people like Jacob, Solomon, and Daniel who heard from God in their dreams. Today, God speaks to us through the Bible, but He could still do it through a dream if He wanted.

Our verses for today have another angel coming with a "behold" message! Joseph had decided to divorce Mary, but he didn't know that God had something different in mind. God sent an angel in a dream to tell Joseph not to go through with divorcing Mary. The angel told him that Mary's baby was created miraculously by the Holy Spirit, and God wanted him to go ahead and marry her. It was all part of God's plan to send Jesus to our world as the promised Savior, and He wanted Joseph to follow His instructions.

But as he considered these things, behold, an angel of the Lord appeared to him in a dream, saying, "Joseph, son of David, do not fear to take Mary as your wife, for that which is conceived in her is from the Holy Spirit. She will bear a son, and you shall call His name Jesus, for He will save His people from their sins." All this took place to fulfill what the Lord had spoken by the prophet: "Behold, the virgin shall conceive and bear a son, and they shall call his name Immanuel" (which means, God with us).
- Matthew 1:20-23

REFLECTION QUESTIONS

1. Why do you think God wanted Joseph to keep his promise to wed Mary?

2. What does it mean that Jesus would save people from their sins?

ACTIVITY

Use posterboard/construction paper and decorating supplies to create megaphones. When God says something, He wants us to listen. Another way to say "behold" is "listen up!" Use the megaphones to share with each other what you've learned so far about God and about Jesus' birth.

DAY 12
INSTANT OBEDIENCE

When your parents tell you to do something, do you listen and obey right away? You might not feel like it if they want you to wash the dishes or make your bed. If what they're telling you is something good like getting in the car so you can go for ice cream, you probably do what they say instantly! Your parents expect that you'll follow their directions. More than that, God expects you to obey your parents. It's part of the commandments He gave us in the Bible to follow.

When Joseph woke from sleep, he did as the angel of the Lord commanded him: he took his wife, but knew her not until she had given birth to a son. And he called His name Jesus.
- Matthew 1:24-25

When God gives instructions, He wants us to pay attention and obey just like with our parents. Mary was visited by the angel, Gabriel, who told her she was going to be the mother of Jesus. After receiving the message, Mary willingly agreed to be part of His plan. Joseph had a similar experience with an angel through a dream. After he woke up, Joseph followed the angel's instructions right away. Mary's and Joseph's response to God reminds us that obeying the Lord, doing everything He desires us to do, is always the right thing. Following God's plan is always for our good and His glory.

REFLECTION QUESTIONS

1. Why should you obey and honor your parents?

2. What does it look like to listen and obey the Lord?

ACTIVITY

Play a game of Simon Says. Everyone should take turns being the leader and the players. As a leader, give clear instructions. As a player, listen carefully and follow the leader's instructions. As our perfect leader, God gives us good instructions for our best and for His glory to be shown through us.

DAY 13

FAMILY TRIP TO BETHLEHEM

And Joseph also went up from Galilee, from the town of Nazareth, to Judea, to the city of David, which is called Bethlehem, because he was of the house and lineage of David, to be registered with Mary, his betrothed, who was with child.
- Luke 2:4-5

Think about who is part of your family. The people who live in your house with you probably pop into your mind first. Then you might go on to include your grandparents, aunts, uncles, and cousins, too. What about your great-grandparents, and your great-great grandparents, and your great-great-great grandparents and so on? They are part of your family, too. The list of generations who lived before you is called your lineage or family line. It can be interesting to find out how far back in history you can trace your relatives.

There was a census, an official counting of people, right before it was time for Jesus to be born. This census required people to travel to the hometown of their family lineage. Mary and Joseph needed to go to Bethlehem to be counted. Bethlehem is known as the city of King David, and their family line traced back to him. This is a very important part of the Christmas story because Old Testament prophecy said a special ruler would come from Bethlehem. God planned out every detail of Jesus' birth that would point to Him as the Messiah, the Savior of the world, even down to the city where He would be born.

REFLECTION QUESTIONS

1. Why do you think family is important to God?

2. Why is your family important to you?

ACTIVITY

Create a family tree together. You can look online to find examples and a template to use. Start with your household, kids and parents. Add grandparents, aunts, uncles, and cousins. Talk to family members to see how far back you can go with your relatives. As you do this, ask your grandparents to share stories about their siblings, parents, and grandparents. If you're able, capture these stories digitally or write them down to go with your family tree.

DAY 14
PERFECT TIMING

When you must wait for something good, it's difficult. For example, you might feel like time goes by very slowly while you're waiting to celebrate your birthday. And then there's Christmas! As you look around at decorations going up, hear Christmas music everywhere, and shop for gifts, you get more and more excited. Waiting for December 25th to come is tough because it's such a special day. Even though it's difficult to wait, you know exactly when your birthday and Christmas are going to happen.

> But when the fullness of time had come, God sent forth His Son, born of woman, born under the law...
> - Galatians 4:4

God gave Old Testament prophets messages about Jesus' birth. The people knew the Messiah, God's chosen one, was coming, but they didn't know when. It was just in the future at some moment. For the Israelites, patiently waiting was probably difficult, and they may have thought from time to time that God was taking too long to keep His promise in sending the Messiah. There is an important phrase in today's verse about when Jesus would come – "in the fullness of time." It means that God had planned a specific time to send Jesus. What we need to remember is no matter how long we have to wait, God's timing is perfect, and He answers our prayers at just the right moment.

REFLECTION QUESTIONS

1. How do you think the people felt as they waited for Jesus to come?

2. Why is God's perfect timing always best?

ACTIVITY

There are 11 more days until Christmas. Create a special activity countdown while you're waiting. You'll need 11 envelopes and some paper or blank cards. On the outside of the envelope, starting with December 15th, write each date through December 25th. As a family, think of 11 activities and write them each on the paper or card. You might include things like taking a nighttime drive to look at Christmas lights or donating toys for kids in need. For Christmas Day, choose an activity to do to honor Jesus. Open one envelope each day and do what you've written.

DAY 15
A DIFFERENT KIND OF KING

> And while they were there, the time came for her to give birth. And she gave birth to her firstborn son and wrapped Him in swaddling cloths and laid Him in a manger, because there was no place for them in the inn.
> - Luke 2:6-7

You, along with many people, were likely born in a hospital where nurses and doctors took care of your mom and you. The location was clean and safe but probably not super fancy. Think about a king whose birth and life is very different from yours. A king would be born somewhere grand with all the best of everything. A king lives in a fancy castle and has lots of money. A king is the most important person in all the land and is in charge of everyone who lives in the kingdom.

When Mary gave birth to Jesus, there wasn't a nice place to stay in crowded Bethlehem. Instead, they were offered a place where animals lived, probably a dirty and stinky place. The bed where Mary laid Jesus was normally used for animals' food. As for riches, His family didn't have much, and they lived very humbly. Nothing about Jesus' life was like a king's should be, but this was part of God's plan. Jesus came to establish a different kind of kingdom, an upside-down kingdom, where He would spend time with people no one else would, serve others instead of being served, and create a kingdom that would never end.

REFLECTION QUESTIONS

1. What do you think of the place where Jesus was born?

2. How does Jesus' kind of kingdom differ from any other type of kingdom?

ACTIVITY

Play the Upside-Down Cup Game. You'll need about a dozen plastic cups and a timer to play. Divide into two teams. If your family is small, you could invite others to join you. Put the plastic cups in the middle of the room, half of them right-side up and half upside-down. Teams gather on opposite sides of the room. One team will be the upside-downers; the other will be the right-side uppers. Set the timer for 5 minutes. At the same time, the teams try to get as many cups as they can to match the direction of their team's name. When the timer goes off, the team with the most cups in the right direction wins.

DAY 16
A MOST EXCITING ANNOUNCEMENT

And in the same region there were shepherds out in the field, keeping watch over their flock by night. And an angel of the Lord appeared to them, and the glory of the Lord shone around them, and they were filled with great fear. And the angel said to them, "Fear not, for behold, I bring you good news of great joy that will be for all the people. For unto you is born this day in the city of David a Savior, who is Christ the Lord. And this will be a sign for you: you will find a baby wrapped in swaddling cloths and lying in a manger."
- Luke 2:8-12

Have you ever watched a sporting event on TV? Each team has its own official announcers who talk about all kinds of things during the game, but when there's a fantastic play on the field, you definitely can't miss it by the way they communicate. Excitement fills their voices, and the volume goes way up!

On the night Jesus was born, God shared the outstanding news with a group of shepherds by sending one of His angels with a "Behold!" message. The sky was dark, and everything was quiet except for the sounds of the sheep when suddenly the angel appeared with the brightness of God's glory surrounding him. This was a birth announcement unlike any that had been or ever will be. It was exciting, important, and joyful news that wasn't just for a few people but for everyone, including you! Jesus came to make a way for all people who believe in Him to have their sins forgiven and to become part of God's family forever!

REFLECTION QUESTIONS

1. Why do you think God sent an angel to announce Jesus' birth?

2. What do you imagine the glory of God looks like?

ACTIVITY

The glory of the Lord must be the most brilliant sight to see! Each family member will be on the lookout for things you see around you that are bright and shining, like the sunrise or Christmas decorations. As you find them, take a picture. After collecting photos, sit down as a family and look through them. Imagine together how much more magnificent God's glory must be!

DAY 17

FILLED WITH WONDER

If you discover something in nature you've never seen before, does it make you curious to find out what it is? Another word to use in place of curiosity is "wonder." There are questions to wonder about, like "Where do waves come from?" or "Where do birds go when it's raining?" Wonder can also be a feeling of surprise caused by something beautiful, unexpected, or indescribable. When you see a magnificent sunset with so many amazing colors in the sky, you might look at it with wonder at the beauty of God's creation.

And they went with haste and found Mary and Joseph, and the baby lying in a manger. And when they saw it, they made known the saying that had been told them concerning this child. And all who heard it wondered at what the shepherds told them.
- Luke 2:16-18

The story of Christmas is filled with wonder, both the questioning kind and the awesome feeling kind. The shepherds' wonder led them to leave the field and their sheep to go and find this special baby. After meeting Him, they spread the news to people all around about the marvelous things they had heard and seen. Everyone they told wondered about what the shepherds said. Some may have been filled with questions like "Are they making this up?" or "Could this baby really be the promised Savior?" Then there were those who stood in wonder, marveling at the surprising and exciting news that Jesus, the Messiah, had finally come!

REFLECTION QUESTIONS

1. If you were one of the shepherds who met Jesus as a baby, what would you tell people about Him?

2. What is something you've seen or heard that fills you with wonder?

ACTIVITY

Go on a walk to find things that fill you with wonder. Notice the plants, animals, and trees around you. See the buildings and vehicles God gave people the ability to design and construct. With familiar things, look very closely to discover details you haven't seen that show just how awesome God's creation is. Thank God for creating so many wonderful things!

DAY 18
WHAT THE WISE MEN KNEW

Now after Jesus was born in Bethlehem of Judea in the days of Herod the king, behold, wise men from the east came to Jerusalem, saying, "Where is He who has been born King of the Jews? For we saw His star when it rose and have come to worship Him."
- Matthew 2:1-2

Have you ever been called on at school to answer one of your teacher's questions? It can be an uncomfortable feeling. Maybe your hands get sweaty, your face turns red, and your stomach flip flops all over the place if you don't know the answer. What about times when you were certain you had the right answer? You probably gave the correct response without the sweaty hands, red face, or butterflies in your stomach. You were confident.

Wise men in the Bible were people who had a lot of answers to hard questions. They studied all kinds of subjects like history, astronomy, and law. In fact, they were so smart that important people like kings would call on them to help with their questions and problems. The wise men in the Christmas story were likely a lot like others in the Bible. We don't know exactly how they gathered information about the God of the Israelites or even if they followed Him, but the coolest thing is that somehow, they were confident about the message of the star. They knew beyond a shadow of a doubt that the star belonged to the King of the Jews, and their desire was to find Him and worship Him.

REFLECTION QUESTIONS

1. Why do you think the wise men were searching for Jesus?

2. How do you think the wise men knew Jesus was the King of the Jews?

ACTIVITY

If you have a nativity set with the baby Jesus in it, you can use that figure for this game. If not, you can use a small doll or paper drawing of a baby. Like the wise men traveled to find Jesus, you're going to try to find Him in your own home. Take turns hiding baby Jesus somewhere in your house. Have everyone else search for it. The person who hid the figure can give hints along the way, kind of like the star helped the wise men. Once someone finds it, they become the hider, and the rest of the family tries to find baby Jesus.

DAY 19
FOLLOW THAT STAR

When your family goes on a trip to a new place, what do your parents use to know how to get there? They use a map app. It's really handy because all you have to do is enter your current location and the location of your destination, and a voice on the app gives you the directions step by step. Map apps make it so easy for people to travel from one place to another.

After listening to the king, they went on their way. And behold, the star that they had seen when it rose went before them until it came to rest over the place where the child was. When they saw the star, they rejoiced exceedingly with great joy.
- Matthew 2:9-10

The wise men didn't have an app to help them find Jesus, but they did have something a lot cooler – a star! When they saw the star at home, they decided to travel to Jerusalem, the capital city of Israel, to see if that's where the new King was. In Jerusalem, they spoke with King Herod to see if he knew where to find the new King. Herod consulted his own wise men who told him the prophecy said Jesus would be from Bethlehem, so that's where he sent them. After leaving Herod, the wise men saw the star again, and they were so excited and joyful. The star was there to lead them directly to the house where they found who they'd been searching for!

REFLECTION QUESTIONS

1. Why do you think God used a star to lead the wise men to Jesus?

2. Why did the reappearance of the star fill the wise men with joy?

ACTIVITY

For this game, you need some candy or small $1 fun items and a flashlight. Choose someone to go first and have them cover their eyes or leave the room. Hide one of the treats for them. After it's hidden, turn the lights off in the room. Using the flashlight, lead the person on a journey around the room until you come to the place where the treat is hidden. Shine the light directly on the spot for them to find their treat. Repeat for everyone in the family until your treats run out.

DAY 20
WORSHIP THE KING

When you hear the word "worship," what do you think of? Like most people, you probably think of singing. You're not wrong, but there is so much more to worship than singing for God. Worship also includes serving others, prayer, and reading His Word. It looks like spending time quietly in awe of the amazing, powerful, and loving God He is. Sometimes, when we think about how magnificent God is, we can't help but bow before Him.

And going into the house, they saw the child with Mary His mother, and they fell down and worshiped Him. Then, opening their treasures, they offered Him gifts, gold and frankincense and myrrh.
- Matthew 2:11

As soon as the wise men saw Jesus, they fell down in worship of Him. Bowing before the Lord showed Him respect and honor. It communicated an adoration for Him. As a sign of the wise men recognizing Jesus as the King, they also brought Him special gifts. They gave Him gold, a precious metal that represented Jesus' kingship. They gave Him frankincense, an expensive perfume that acknowledged Him as God. Finally, they gave Jesus myrrh, another expensive perfume used to put on bodies to prepare them for burial. Myrrh represented Jesus' death to take away the sins of the world. Just like the wise men honored Jesus because of who He was, we should spend time worshipping the King of Kings, the Messiah, and the Savior of the world, too.

REFLECTION QUESTIONS

1. Why did the wise men fall down in worship when they saw Jesus?

2. What are some ways you can worship the Lord?

ACTIVITY

Put on your favorite worship music and spend some time in awe of Jesus. You might want to kneel or lay face down on the ground like the wise men did to honor and show your love for Him. You can pray out loud or silently, sing along with the music or listen to it, or simply tell Jesus how you feel about Him quietly in your heart. It is good for us to give the Lord all the glory and love He deserves.

DAY 21

DANGER!

At school, you have fire drills to help everyone practice what to do in case of a real fire. During a drill, you get to hear what the fire alarm sounds like. It's really loud! An alarm needs to be loud so students and teachers know there's danger nearby. Then, you and your classmates follow the teachers' instructions quickly, carefully, and quietly, and no one goes back into the school building until the adults in charge say it's safe.

Now when they had departed, behold, an angel of the Lord appeared to Joseph in a dream and said, "Rise, take the child and His mother, and flee to Egypt, and remain there until I tell you, for Herod is about to search for the child, to destroy Him." And he rose and took the child and His mother by night and departed to Egypt and remained there until the death of Herod. This was to fulfill what the Lord had spoken by the prophet, "Out of Egypt I called my Son."
- Matthew 2:13-15

After the wise men left to return to their home, Joseph had another important dream from God where an angel spoke to him about something very important. This time, like a fire alarm, it was a message that danger was near. King Herod wanted to find Jesus and kill Him! The angel gave Joseph instructions about what to do, where to go, and when it would be safe to come back. Joseph listened carefully so he could do everything God told him. He didn't spend days thinking about going to Egypt. He didn't ask other people what they thought he should do. Joseph listened to the angel of the Lord and did exactly what he was told. He was obedient to God's message.

REFLECTION QUESTIONS

1. Why do you think King Herod wanted to destroy Jesus?

2. What are some things God says in the Bible to keep you safe?

ACTIVITY

You'll need a blindfold and soft pillows for this activity. Pick a room to play in and a person to go first. While the first player waits in another room, arrange pillows as obstacles between one side of the room and the other. Then, blindfold the first player and lead him or her to one side of the room. Give the player detailed directions for crossing the room without stepping on any obstacles. The player has to try to follow the directions to make it across the room. The only additional help you can give is to say, "Danger!" every time the player gets too close to an obstacle. Play again with a new arrangement of obstacles and a new player.

DAY 22

THE BEST GIFTS

One of the most fun parts of Christmas is receiving gifts. You might even start writing a list of things you want for Christmas months ahead of time. Then you have to try to be patient as you wait for what seems like forever to open your presents. Something that's just as fun as getting presents is giving them. As you make presents at school or home for the people you love or go to the store to buy things for them, you often think about how much they'll enjoy their gifts. It's all very exciting!

Now there are varieties of gifts, but the same Spirit; and there are varieties of service, but the same Lord; and there are varieties of activities, but it is the same God who empowers them all in everyone.
- 1 Corinthians 12:4-6

God loves to give us good gifts, too. In fact, there are different spiritual gifts God gives those who love and follow Him. These presents aren't physical items, like a game or craft kit; they're gifts meant to help us encourage others in a godly way. Your gift might be the natural ability to be compassionate and serve others, demonstrating God's love and care. Or perhaps you are a really good teacher who is able to explain God's Word in ways others can easily understand. Whatever it is, God gives you the power to use the gift He gives you to bring glory to Him and to bless others with His goodness.

REFLECTION QUESTIONS

1. What do you think are some of the special gifts God gives to those who love and follow Him?

2. Why does God give different people different gifts?

ACTIVITY

Sometimes, we need help to figure out a spiritual gift God has given us. As a family, talk about the special gifts from God that you see in each other. Discuss ways you can use these gifts to help other people. Pray together to thank God for these gifts and ask Him to teach you how to use them to give Him glory.

DAY 23
FOREVER LOVED

Love is patient and kind. It's happy when you're happy and sad when you're sad. Love encourages, protects, and wants the very best for you. God's love is like this but even bigger than any human kind of love. He shows His love for all people, including you, throughout the Bible, and there's one big story that displays His forever love.

> Give thanks to the Lord, for He is good, for His steadfast love endures forever.
> - Psalm 136:1

God created a perfect world. He made Adam and Eve to be part of His family. Then God's enemy, Satan, lied to Adam and Eve, and they chose to follow a lie instead of God's truth. They sinned. Because sin is so bad and God is so good, Adam, Eve, and everyone to come couldn't live in the beautiful garden in perfect relationship with God. No matter how hard people tried to take care of their sin problem, they couldn't. We all need a rescuer to provide a way back into a relationship with God. So, God sent Jesus to the world to die as the perfect sacrifice for sin and to be raised back to life again. Now that Jesus has conquered sin, every person who believes He is God's Son and asks Him to take away their sins can become part of God's family forever. That is what God's never-ending love looks like.

REFLECTION QUESTIONS

1. When you disobey God and sin, what are some consequences you experience?

2. What does it feel like knowing Jesus can forgive your sins so you can be part of God's family?

ACTIVITY

Grab a piece of poster board or large fancy paper and some markers or crayons to create a big thank you card for God. Decorate the front and write a note inside about who God is, what He's done, and why you're thankful for His love. Sign your card and place it under the tree as a gift for the Lord.

DAY 24

BACK TO THE BEGINNING

> In those days a decree went out from Caesar Augustus that all the world should be registered. This was the first registration when Quirinius was governor of Syria. And all went to be registered, each to his own town.
> - Luke 2:1-3

You might wonder sometimes why your parents or teachers tell you certain things over and over again. They're not trying to annoy you; they're trying to help you remember important stuff. Repetition makes it easier for your brain to recall what you've learned. It helps your brain put information into long-term storage so it's harder to forget. The best part of remembering things is sharing what you know with others.

Out of all the things you could learn about, God's Word is the most important. Today's verses go back to the beginning of the Christmas story. Here's the speedy-quick, super short retelling: An angel told Mary she was going to have a special baby who would be the Savior of the world. An angel told Joseph to go ahead and marry Mary. They traveled to Bethlehem right before Mary gave birth to Jesus. They couldn't find a place with any room to stay, so Jesus was born and laid in a manger. An angel told some shepherds about Jesus. The shepherds ran to see Him. Later, wise men from far away came to worship the King of the Jews. They left, and an angel warned Joseph to get Jesus to safety. Joseph obeyed. All was well.

REFLECTION QUESTIONS

1. What is one new thing you've learned about the story of Christmas?

2. How can you share what you've learned with others?

ACTIVITY

Christmas is such an important part of God's entire story in the Bible, and it's something we definitely should remember. If you've been making stick puppet characters since Day 10, you can use them for this activity. If not, you can use a nativity set. Think back to the very beginning of the Christmas story. See if you can act it out together using the characters. If you have a hard time remembering, look back over the Bible verses for each day's devotion to help.

DAY 25
CHRISTMAS DAY!

Today is the day! Christmas is finally here! Aren't you excited? After waiting so long, you can open your presents and give your gifts. You'll probably listen to Christmas songs and eat some yummy food. Maybe you'll visit your grandparents and aunts and uncles or get together with close family friends. You'll smile for lots of pictures, too. What a spectacular celebration!

"For unto you is born this day in the city of David a Savior, who is Christ the Lord. And this will be a sign for you: you will find a baby wrapped in swaddling cloths and lying in a manger." And suddenly there was with the angel a multitude of the heavenly host praising God and saying, "Glory to God in the highest, and on earth peace among those with whom He is pleased!"
- Luke 2:11-14

In the midst of everything going on today, stop and take some time to think about the reason we celebrate. Today's verses are some of the most familiar ones related to Christmas. It's the best birth announcement of all time. When the angel appeared to the shepherds to share the news of Jesus' birth, he told them exactly who this special baby was – the Savior, Christ the Lord. Then, the most wonderful thing happened...the sky filled up with angels praising the Lord! It had to have been such a breathtaking sight to behold. Although the birth of a new baby is always something to celebrate, no infant, past or future, will receive a welcome like the one Jesus did. He is worthy of all the praise and glory we can give Him. "Glory to God in the Highest!"

REFLECTION QUESTIONS

1. What would it have been like to hear all those angels praising God?

2. What is so important about the Christmas story?

ACTIVITY

At some point in the day, revisit the thank you card you made for the Lord. Think about everything you've learned and done as you've read through this devotional. Talk about your favorite parts of the Christmas story. Spend a few moments to BEHOLD the Savior, the Son of God, the Messiah, Immanuel.

HOW TO KNOW JESUS

Whether you're reading this and have never started a relationship with Jesus or you do have a relationship with Him and want to know how you can tell your friends about Him, this page is for you!

IN THE BEGINNING

First, God is the Creator (Genesis 1:1). He created everything, even you. Second, God is perfect in all His ways (Psalm 18:30). So, combined, that makes God the Perfect Creator of all things. He is in charge of everything, and He is 100% right.

OUR SIN PROBLEM

God is the perfect King, and when we think, do, or say something that goes against His ways, it's called sin. And because God is who He is, all sin is purposely disobeying Him (Psalm 51:3-4). The consequence for our disobedience is death (Romans 6:23). Our physical bodies get sick and die, and the spiritual part of us, our inside beliefs and feelings, dies, too. We can't take care of our sin problem by ourselves, no matter how hard we try.

JESUS IS THE BEST GIFT EVER

Jesus is God's Son, sent to earth to live a perfect life. He was God's gift to us. He never sinned, which meant He was the only one who could fix our sin problem once-and-for-all (Matthew 1:18-21). Jesus died on the cross and then came back to life to save everyone who believes in Him from their sins (John 3:16). Only Jesus could do this.

If you want to have your sins forgiven and become part of God's family, there are some things you need to do:

ADMIT

First, you need to admit that you sin and that you cannot fix your relationship with God on your own.

BELIEVE

Next, believe that Jesus is who He says He is – God's Son who died on the cross and was raised back to life again in order to take care of our sin problem.

CONFESS

Finally, talk to Jesus and say that you are a sinner and need Him to take away your sins, which is forgiveness (1 John 1:9).

After you've done these things, you are a part of God's family forever. You're a new creation (2 Cor. 5:17)! God loves you and wants to teach you more about Him, how to love Him, and how to be more like Him. You can get to know Him better by reading your Bible, praying, listening to Him, and learning together with your family and others at church.